Dirk Nowitzki

By Jeffrey Zuehlke

AMAZING
ATHLETES

 Lerner Publications Company • Minneapolis

For Graham, Tall Teuton

Lerner Publications Company
A division of Lerner Publishing Group, Inc.
241 First Avenue North
Minneapolis, MN 55401 U.S.A.

Website address: www.lernerbooks.com

Library of Congress Cataloging-in-Publication Data

Zuehlke, Jeffrey, 1968–
    Dirk Nowitzki / by Jeffrey Zuehlke.
      p.   cm. — (Amazing athletes)
    Includes bibliographical references and index.
    ISBN-13: 978-0-8225-7661-7 (lib. bdg. : alk. paper)
    1. Nowitzki, Dirk, 1978– —Juvenile literature. 2. Basketball players—United States—Biography—
Juvenile literature. 3. Nowitzki, Dirk, 1978– 4. Basketball players—United States—Biography.
I. Title.
GV884.N69 Z84 2008
796.323092—dc22 [B]   2006100867

Manufactured in the United States of America
1 2 3 4 5 6 – DP – 13 12 11 10 09 08

TABLE OF CONTENTS

The Mavericks played tough defense during game seven of the **Western Conference Semifinals.**

MOST VALUABLE PLAYER

The Dallas Mavericks were in trouble. They were battling the San Antonio Spurs. It was game seven of the 2006 National Basketball Association (NBA) Western Conference Semifinals. If the Mavs lost this **playoff** game, their season would be over.

The game had started out great for the Mavs. Led by their superstar **forward** Dirk Nowitzki, the Mavs had built up a 20-point lead. But the Spurs were a tough team. They had won the NBA championship in 2005.

Sure enough, the Spurs charged back. With a minute left, they tied the game at 101. With just 32 seconds left in the game, Spurs **guard** Manu Ginobli hit a **three-point basket**. The Spurs were leading, 104–101!

San Antonio Spurs' star Tim Duncan *(right)* watches the ball fall through the net. Duncan scored 41 points in this game.

The Mavs needed to score. They turned to their leader and best player—Dirk Nowitzki. Mavs guard Jason Terry dribbled the ball up the court. Dirk called for the ball and took the pass. Spurs player Bruce Bowen pounced on Dirk. But the Mavs forward dribbled and spun away from Bowen. Then Dirk drove to the basket. Ginobli ran up to try to knock the ball away. But Dirk couldn't be stopped.

The ball rolled into the basket as Ginobli slapped Dirk on the wrist. Two points! And

Manu Ginobli hits Dirk on the wrist as the Mavs forward jumps for the basket.

Dirk pumps his fist after sinking the free throw that tied the score at 104.

Ginobli had **fouled** Dirk. The Mavs superstar could tie the game with a **free throw**!

The pressure was on. If Dirk missed, the Mavs season might be over. Could he do it?

Dirk calmly stepped to the free throw line. He ran his fingers through his mop of shaggy blond hair. He flipped the ball into the air and through the basket. The game was tied at 104 with just over 21 seconds left.

As a scorer, Dirk is almost impossible to stop. "The players who are as big as Dirk aren't quick enough to guard him," says former Mavs coach Don Nelson. "The players who are as quick as Dirk aren't big enough to guard him."

The Spurs had one more chance to score. But they couldn't get it done. The game went into **overtime**. The teams would fight it out for five more minutes to decide the winner.

The battle continued. Dirk started out by making a great pass to teammate Josh Howard. Howard slipped the ball into the basket for two points. The Mavs had the lead! The Spurs fought back, but they couldn't keep up with the Mavs. Dallas won, 119–111. Dirk had played an incredible game. He had scored 37 points and grabbed 15 **rebounds**.

Afterward, Mavs players praised their leader. "It seemed like everybody did something special tonight and it started with Dirk," said guard Jerry Stackhouse. "Dirk definitely played like an MVP [most valuable player]," added guard Devin Harris. "He played out of his mind. He did everything he needed to do to ensure victory and then more. He's our MVP."

Dirk celebrates the Mavs' victory over the Spurs as he exits the court in San Antonio.

Wurzburg, where Dirk was born, is located near the center of Germany.

LATE STARTER

Dirk Werner Nowitzki was born June 19, 1978, in Wurzburg, Germany. He comes from a family of talented athletes. Dirk's father, Joerg, plays and coaches a game called team handball. Dirk's mother, Helga, played basketball on the German national team. Even Dirk's older sister, Silke, is a talented basketball player.

Soccer is the most popular sport in Germany. Dirk grew up playing soccer and team handball. "I didn't start basketball until I was 12 or 13," Dirk says. But once he tried out the game, he found he was very good at it.

By the time he was 16, Dirk was playing for his hometown's professional team, the Wurzburg X-Rays. His skills caught the attention of a local basketball coach, Holger Geschwindner. The coach saw that Dirk had the talent to be a great player. But he knew that Dirk had a lot to learn.

As a youngster, Dirk wasn't interested in doing his schoolwork. But his coach, Holger Geschwindner, told him that he had to practice with his mind as well as his body. "If you want to be a good player," he told Dirk, "you have to learn how to learn."

Geschwindner offered to coach Dirk. "I can make your son the best player in Germany," he told Dirk's parents. "And he can play in the NBA if he will commit to working with me."

The Nowitzkis agreed. Dirk was eager to learn. He and his coach spent hours and hours practicing. "Without [Geschwindner], I wouldn't be where I am," says Dirk. "He taught me how to shoot, how to move, how to play. I owe him everything. He is like a second dad."

Dirk's play kept getting better. He perfected his

Holger Geschwindner taught Dirk many of the basketball skills that he uses in the NBA.

shooting. He worked hard on his rebounding. In March 1998, he and several other European players were invited to show off their talent in the United States. Nineteen-year-old Dirk flew to San Antonio, Texas, to play in the Nike Hoops Summit game. He and his teammates played against a team of top American high school players.

Each year, talented young basketball players from around the world play in the Nike Hoops Summit.

Dirk was the star of the game. He scored 33 points and grabbed 14 rebounds. He also made 19 of 23 free throws. Dirk's incredible play caught the attention of many NBA teams. A few months later, Dirk was selected in the NBA **draft**. He would play for the Dallas Mavericks.

Dirk was shocked when he heard the news. He didn't feel he was ready to play in the NBA yet. He still had so much to learn. "I wasn't sure if I really wanted to go," he said.

Steve Nash *(wearing number 13)* was already a star when Dirk joined the Mavs.

TAKING OFF

Despite his worries, Dirk accepted the challenge of the NBA. He joined a Dallas team that already had two great players—guards Steve Nash and Michael Finley. Would Dirk be good enough to play alongside them?

After a bad game, Dirk works extra hard to improve. "He has a key to the gym, and if he has a bad game, he comes back that night to shoot," says Mavs owner Mark Cuban.

Dirk struggled at first. NBA players were much bigger, stronger, and faster than the players he had faced in Germany. At seven feet, Dirk was one of the league's tallest players. But he was very skinny. The big NBA players could push him around easily.

But Dirk's teammates supported him. "He was so down on himself," says Nash. "There were a lot of times when I would have to pump him up." Dirk and Nash spent hours working on their skills together. The two became best friends.

By his second season, Dirk was starting to catch on. He put up strong scoring and rebounding numbers. He averaged more than 17 points and 6 rebounds per game. He finished second in the voting for the NBA's Most Improved Player award.

As Dirk started to play well in the NBA, he became more popular with fans.

Dirk, Nash, and Finley were making the high-scoring Mavs an exciting team to watch. The 2000–2001 season was a great year for Dirk and his team. Dirk averaged nearly 22 points and just over 9 rebounds per game. He was named to the **All-NBA Team**.

The Mavs won 53 games and made it to the playoffs for the first time in years. They defeated the Utah Jazz in an exciting first round series. But they lost to the San Antonio Spurs in the Western Conference Semifinals.

Dirk puts up a shot against Utah in the first round of the 2000–2001 playoffs.

The Mavs wanted to keep Dirk on the team for a long time. They made him a very rich man.

BETTER AND BETTER

The Mavs knew that Dirk was their star of the future. Before the 2001–2002 season, they signed him to a huge **contract**. Dirk agreed to play for the Mavs for the next six seasons. The Mavs would pay him $79 million!

Dirk loves music. He can often be found listening to his iPod. One of Dirk's favorite hobbies is playing the saxophone.

Dirk earned his big money with fantastic play. He averaged more than 23 points a game. He grabbed nearly 10 rebounds per game. He was also selected to play in his first NBA All-Star game for the Western Conference.

Steve Nash praised his teammate and best friend. "[Dirk's] always getting better," he said. "When he arrived in Dallas, we didn't know if he could play with us. Now we ask ourselves if we're good enough to play with him."

Dirk and Nash powered the Mavs to another great season. The team won 57 games and made it to the semifinals again. But they could not get past the Spurs.

Dirk's fifth season was his best yet. In 2002–2003, he upped his scoring average to more than 25 points a game. He was again named to the NBA All-Star team.

By this time, the Mavs had become one of the NBA's powerhouse teams. They dazzled fans with their exciting, high-scoring style of play. Dirk, Nash, and Finley were the team's leaders and best players. They earned the nickname the Big Three.

Steve Nash *(left)*, Dirk *(center)*, and Michael Finley *(right)* made the Mavs an exciting team to watch.

The Mavs won a whopping 60 games during the 2002–2003 season. In the playoffs, they blasted their way to the Western Conference Finals. Dirk's team lost to the Spurs in six games.

Losing to the Spurs was tough. But the 2003–2004 season was even tougher. Although the Mavs won 52 games, they lost in the first round of the playoffs.

Dirk was frustrated. But he believed the Big Three could still bring a championship to Dallas.

Dirk and Nash look on from the bench as the Mavs lose in the first round of the 2003–2004 playoffs.

Steve Nash left the Mavs after the 2003–2004 season to join the Phoenix Suns.

TEAM LEADER

Sadly, the Big Three would never get a chance to win it all. Before the 2004–2005 season, Steve Nash signed a contract to play for the Phoenix Suns. The Big Three was no more.

Dirk takes most of his shots from far away, but he has learned to score close to the basket as well.

Dirk was upset that the Mavs had let his best friend leave. He knew he would have to play even better to keep Dallas near the top.

Dirk was ready for the challenge. He boosted his scoring average to 26 points per game. Earlier in his career, Dirk scored mostly with **jump shots**. But by this time, he had learned other ways to score. He wasn't afraid to take on the big players close to the basket. "I've never seen Dirk play better," said Mavs coach Don Nelson.

The other Mavs players looked to him for leadership. "Dirk has been a great leader," said his teammate, Devin Harris. "He's always encouraging you. If you make a mistake, he's the first one to come tell you it's okay."

Dirk doesn't smile much on the court. But he has a great sense of humor off of it. "He's never serious. He's always joking around," says Steve Nash.

The Mavs won 58 games. But once again, Dirk and his teammates couldn't get it done in the playoffs. They lost to the Phoenix Suns in the conference semifinals.

In 2005–2006, Dirk averaged more than 26 points per game. He was selected to the Western Conference All-Star team for the fifth straight year. Dirk also finished third in the voting for the NBA Most Valuable Player Award. He had become a superstar and one of the game's best players.

The Mavs could not get past Dwyane Wade and the Miami Heat in the NBA Finals.

The Mavs won 60 games and cruised into the playoffs. In the first round, they crushed the Memphis Grizzlies in four games. Then Dirk led his team to victory in a tough seven-game series against the San Antonio Spurs. In the Western Conference Finals, Dirk's 50 points in game five helped the Mavs knock off the Suns. Dirk and the Mavs had reached the NBA Finals! They would play the Miami Heat.

But the Mavs couldn't beat the Heat. Miami stars Shaquille O'Neal and Dwyane Wade were too tough. The Mavs lost the series in six games. It was a disappointing end to a great season.

The Mavs started out the 2006–2007 season with four straight losses. But Dirk and the Mavs were not about to give up. They caught fire and won the next 12 games in a row. A 13-game win streak followed. The Mavs won every single game they played in February 2007. Dirk and the Mavericks rolled into the playoffs but lost to the Golden State Warriors in the first round. But Dirk soon had good news. He had won the NBA Most Valuable Player Award.

Dirk started his pro career as a skinny kid. He could barely hold his own against NBA players. But he has become one of the NBA's best. How does he do it? He never stops working to get better. He even works hard in the **off-season**. "Every season, I want some part of my game to be better than it was the year before," he says. "I'll do anything to get better. That's what this is all about, isn't it?"

Dirk receives the NBA's Most Valuable Player Award for the 2006–2007 season.

Selected Career Highlights

2006–2007   Named NBA Most Valuable Player
Named to Western Conference All-Star team for
  the sixth time

2005–2006   Named to All-NBA first team
Named to the Western Conference All-Star team for the
  fifth time
Finished third in voting for NBA Most Valuable Player
Led Mavericks to the NBA Finals for the first time
Named Western Conference player of the month for
  December 2005
Won 2006 Three-Point Shootout contest at the 2006
  NBA All-Star Game
Scored a season-high 51 points against the Golden State
  Warriors

2004–2005   Named to the Western Conference All-Star team for
  the fourth time
Scored a career-high 53 points in a game against the Houston
  Rockets

2003–2004   Led the Mavericks in scoring average with 21.8 points per game
Led the Mavericks in rebounds per game with 8.7
Named to the Western Conference All-Star team for the third time
Mavericks' leading scorer in 37 games
Mavericks' leading rebounder in 32 games
Made a career-high 8 three-point baskets in a game against
  the Seattle Supersonics

2002–2003   Led the Mavericks in scoring average with 25.1 points per game
Led the Mavericks in rebounds per game with 9.9
Mavericks leading scorer in 50 games
Named to the Western Conference All-Star team for the second
  time

2001–2002   Grabbed a career-high 23 rebounds in a game against the
  Boston Celtics
Led the Mavericks in scoring average with 23.4 points per game
Led the Mavericks in rebounds per game with 9.9
Mavericks leading scorer in 40 games
Mavericks leading rebounder in 44 games
Named to the Western Conference All-Star team for the first time

2000–2001	Named to All-NBA team for the first time
	Led the Mavericks in scoring average with 21.8 points per game
	Led the Mavericks in rebounds per game with 9.2
	Scored 10 or more points in 80 games
	Started all 82 regular season games
1999–2000	Finished second in voting for NBA's Most Improved Player
	Averaged 17.5 points and 6.5 rebounds per game
	Played in all 82 regular season games
1998–1999	Averaged 8.2 points and 3.4 rebounds per game
	Scored a season-high 29 points in a game against the Phoenix Suns

Glossary

All-NBA Team: a team of the best 15 players in the NBA. The All-NBA Team is chosen at the end of each NBA season.

contract: a written deal signed by a player and a team. The player agrees to play for a team for a stated number of years. The team agrees to pay the player a stated amount of money.

draft: a yearly event in which professional teams in a sport are given the chance to pick new players from a selected group

forward: a player on a basketball team who usually plays close to the basket. Forwards need to rebound and shoot the ball well.

fouled: to be hit, touched, or pushed by an opponent in a way that is against the rules

free throw: a one-point shot taken from behind the free throw line. Players often get to shoot free throws after being fouled.

guard: a player on a basketball team whose main job is to handle the ball. Guards need to be good passers and good shooters.

jump shots: plays in which the player jumps and shoots the ball at a distance from the basket

off-season: the time between seasons

overtime: extra time played to decide the winner of a game

playoff: one of a series of contests played after the regular season has ended. Teams compete to become the champion.

rebounds: grabbing the ball after a missed shot or the ball that bounces back after a missed shot

semifinals: the second round of the NBA playoffs. The winner of the semifinals series goes on to the conference finals.

three-point basket: a long-range shot that counts for three points

Western Conference: one of two conferences that make up the NBA. The 15-team Western Conference includes the Dallas Mavericks, San Antonio Spurs, Los Angeles Lakers, and Phoenix Suns.

Further Reading & Websites

Basketball. New York: DK Publishing, 2005.

Savage, Jeff. *Steve Nash.* Minneapolis: Lerner Publications Company, 2007.

Savage, Jeff. *Dwyane Wade.* Minneapolis: Lerner Publications Company, 2007.

Dirk Nowitzki Fan Site
http://www.41fan.net/en/index.html
Find out the latest news about Dirk's life and career from his official fan site.

Espn.com
http://espn.com
Espn.com covers all the major professional sports, including NBA basketball.

Official Site of the Dallas Mavericks
http://www.nba.com/mavericks
Find out the latest Mavs news from the team's official site.

Sports Illustrated for Kids
http://www.sikids.com
The *Sports Illustrated for Kids* website covers all sports, including basketball.

Index

Photo Acknowledgments

Photographs are used with the permission of: : © Andrew P. Scott/Dallas Morning News/CORBIS, p. 4; © Vernon Bryant/ Dallas Morning News /CORBIS, p. 5; ©AP Photo/ Eric Gay, pp. 6,7; © Erich Schlegel/ Dallas Morning News/ CORBIS, pp. 9, 29; © Witold Skrypczak/SuperStock, p. 10; © Michael Mulvey/ Dallas Morning News/CORBIS, p. 12; © Andy Lyons/Getty Images, p. 13; © AP Photo/Kevork Djansezian, p. 15; © AP Photo/Joerg Sarbach, p. 17; © George Fry/ AFP/Getty Images, p. 18; © AP Photo/ Diether Endlicher, p. 19; © AP Photo/ Elaine Thompson, p. 21; © Jose Luis Villegas/Sacramento Bee/ZUMA Press, p. 22; © AP Photo/Matt York, p. 23; © Hector Amezcua/Sacramento Bee/ ZUMA Press, p. 24; © Robert Seale/The Sporting News/ZUMA Press, p. 26; © AP Photo/Matt Slocum, p. 28.

Cover: © AP Photo/Tony Gutierrez